STEEL RAINBOW

THE LEGENDARY
UNDERGROUND GUIDE
TO BECOMING AN '80s ROCK STAR

Written and Illustrated by
JORDAN HART

LYONS PRESS
Guilford, Connecticut
An imprint of Globe Pequot Press

This book is dedicated to mesh tank tops.

And to Teresa, Mom, Dad, Kristen, and Aaron for always putting up with my antics.

To buy books in quantity for corporate use
or incentives, call **(800) 962-0973**
or e-mail **premiums@GlobePequot.com.**

Lyons Press is an imprint of Globe Pequot Press.

Text designer: Bret Kerr
Layout: Maggie Peterson
Project editor: Ellen Urban

Library of Congress Cataloging-in-Publication Data is available on file.

ISBN 978-0-7627-8073-0

Printed in the United States of America
10 9 8 7 6 5 4 3 2 1

DeLorean furnished by Bill Schafer, Darien, Wisconsin (DeLorean Midwest Connection Car Club)

Trademarked names mentioned in *Steel Rainbow:*
Bands:
AC/DC, Bad Company, The Charlie Daniels Band, Jefferson Airplane, Joe Walsh, Kiss, Led Zeppelin, Mötley Crüe, Phil Collins, Queen, Ratt, Twisted Sister, Van Halen

People:
David Lee Roth, Eddie Van Halen, Elton John, Elvis, Eric Clapton, H.G. Wells, Jimi Hendrix, Kenny Rogers, Little Richard, Mozart, Nikki Sixx, Rick Moranis, Siegfried & Roy

Songs:
Black Sabbath, "Iron Man"; Jimi Hendrix Experience, "Bold as Love"; Jimi Hendrix Experience, "Purple Haze"; Joe Walsh, "Rocky Mountain Way"; Kiss, "Lick It Up"; Mötley Crüe, "Looks That Kill"; Phil Collins, "In the Air Tonight"; Quiet Riot, "Bang Your Head (Metal Health)"; Twisted Sister, "We're Not Gonna Take It"; Van Halen, "Eruption"; Van Halen, "Panama"

Other:
Arby's, Camaro, *Cosmopolitan,* Electric Lady Studios, Electric Ladyland (album), Ferrari, Harley Davidson, *Hustler,* Jacuzzi, Maserati, Schlitz Beer, Spandex, Sturgis, USS *Enterprise,* X-Men

CONTENTS

ORIGIN

Looking back at Hair Metal, one thing is apparent: Every band looked and sounded exactly the same. According to legend, this is because of a secret document written by an anonymous record label in 1984. People in the industry deny it ever existed, but a few guitar store owners and washed-up musicians will tell you something different.

According to them, this text promised anyone who set eyes on it fortune and fame . . . if followed correctly. It was rumored to cover everything from how to write music to how to dress. Some even argue that it is solely responsible for the slew of largely successful yet mildly talented '80s bands, better known as cheap imitations of Van Halen.

In 2011, while perusing a thrift store for old rock 'n' roll records, classic rock connoisseur Jordan Hart found a beat-up copy of Ratt's breakthrough album, *Out of the Cellar,* buried in a discount bin. He already owned this record, but something about this one was special. For some reason he was drawn to it, as if it were illuminated by a beam of light backed by the distant "ahhhhhhh" of a men's choir filling the air.

He picked it up and immediately noticed the album jacket was heavier than usual. As he opened it and removed the vinyl, a thick, beer-stained booklet slid into his hands. The title read, *Steel Rainbow: The Guide to Becoming an '80s Rock Star.* Having heard the legend of the mythical document, Jordan quickly realized it had somehow fallen into his hands.

Knowing that the guide was out of date, he wasn't sure what to do. He considered sliding it back into the album sleeve and walking away (after all, anyone who actually followed it today might end up getting mugged). But he knew he'd be doing all of mankind a huge disservice by ignoring this discovery, so he decided to painstakingly copy the text word by word for all to enjoy.

Here, for the first time ever published, is *Steel Rainbow: The Legendary Underground Guide to Becoming an '80s Rock Star.* Even though the rules are kind of irrelevant (unless you have a time machine or enjoy cross-dressing on the weekends), they are still entertaining to look at and wonder: "What the hell was everyone thinking?"

INTRODUCTION

Congratulations! You have been specifically chosen to become the world's next mega rock star. Your amazing looks, sculpted body, and willingness to do—or wear—anything has put you directly on the path to international fortune and fame.

In this guidebook you'll learn everything you need to know to become one of the most popular musicians on the planet, but there is one caveat: You must implement each and every rule in its entirety. Only following a handful of rules will grant you one-hit-wonder status at best. All of the wisdom in this document has been carefully crafted over the past two years, resulting in a formula that creates the perfect rock star.

Quietly spend the next few weeks memorizing this guide. Know that this document is extremely confidential and must be kept secret. Once you can recite each rule from memory, destroy this hard copy immediately. If it falls into the wrong hands (fat or ugly people), the result could be disastrous.

Welcome to the music industry! All you need to do now is follow the proceeding rules and your face will be pinned up on every chick's bedroom wall in a matter of months.

— Anonymous, 1984

I.

THE BASICS

Believe it or not, there is an exact science to becoming a rock star. Simply being a great musician isn't enough to sell out arenas from Texas to Iceland anymore. In today's scene, how you dress, look, and act are much more important than how you play.

Before you start writing music or performing in public, make sure you and your band learn the basic requirements of becoming international rock icons.

EMULATE VAN HALEN AS MUCH AS POSSIBLE

Van Halen put America back on the rock 'n' roll map. Between Eddie's guitar skills and David Lee Roth's showmanship, the band single-handedly laid the foundation for today's rock music. If you want to make it big, you need to Van Halen-*ize* your band as much as possible. This means dressing, sounding, and acting exactly like them.

Word has it they're on the verge of breaking up, which is great news for you. This will leave a giant void in the music industry for your group to fill. Simply sounding like them will actually be enough to get a record deal. Please refer to the Techniques section of this document (page 79) to find specific tips for turning yourself into the second coming of Eddie or DLR.

LOOK GORGEOUS

Currently, if you want to make it in rock 'n' roll, you need to be beautiful. Not naturally gorgeous? You're in luck. Wearing makeup is totally acceptable these days for rock musicians, a miracle solution to fixing genetic imperfections. Simply cake on foundation, eye shadow, and blush to conceal your general unattractiveness.

Warning: If you're fat, short, or unwilling to have a nose job, you'll have to play bass.

WEAR THE MANDATORY MAKEUP FOR EVERY ROCK STAR

Going out in public without makeup is like playing a guitar without strings. Never leave home without a liberal application of *all* of the following:

1. Foundation
2. Blush
3. Lipstick or lip gloss
4. Eye shadow
5. Eyeliner
6. Mascara
7. Glitter

SMILE ALL THE TIME

Note: The only time you should not smile is during
photo shoots. Look sad or angry instead.

HIRE THE BEST
DENTIST IN THE WORLD

No matter how talented a musician you are, crooked, stained, chipped, gapped, or missing teeth will prevent you from landing a record deal (unless it's a Southern label). Since it's mandatory to smile the entire time you're on stage, investing in a good dentist is highly recommended.

Note: Gross gums, acne, and a double chin are equally bad.

LEAD SINGERS MUST BE BLONDE

SHADES

Platinum Record

Sunlight Vanilla

Angel Nectar

Golden Tear Drops

FACIAL HAIR IS UNACCEPTABLE, UNLESS YOU'RE THE BASS PLAYER

Remember: The bass player is only one step up from the band's caterer anyway.

9

SHOWCASE 75 PERCENT OF YOUR CHEST AT ALL TIMES

In a perfect world, you'd be able to walk around shirtless all the time. But until Arby's loses their stupid "no shirts, no service" rule, you'll have to get a little creative.

Leotard

Mesh Tank Top

Sequin Vest

See-Thru Shirt

WHEN IN DOUBT, USE TIGER PRINT

No matter what the dilemma, tiger print is always the answer. Examples:

Q: What pants should I wear?

A: Tiger print.

Q: What type of interior should my Maserati have?

A: Tiger print.

Q: What color should I paint my house?

A: Tiger print.

Q: What should I name my first illegitimate kid?

A: Tiger Printus.

CARRY AN UNHEALTHY OBSESSION WITH AFRICAN CATS

Quick, stealthy, instinctual, lethal, promiscuous, good-looking—do these traits sound familiar? African cats are the animal kingdom's version of rock stars, so celebrate that connection with nature by placing graphics of their face and skin on everything from jean jackets to amplifiers.

THE COLOR PINK
IS YOUR NEW
BEST FRIEND

Animal print may be the greatest motif ever, but sometimes only a solid color is needed.

That's where pink—animal print's sidekick—comes in. Formerly considered to be only a girl's color, pink's vibrant hue hypnotizes everyone around you, convincing people to believe anything you say.

DID YOU KNOW?

The color pink has been proven to instantly turn women on.

ALWAYS CARRY A POCKET MIRROR FOR TWO REASONS: CHECKING YOUR APPEARANCE AND RECREATIONAL USE

MAKE USE OF TRIPLE EXCLAMATION POINTS EVERYWHERE!!!

Imagine landing a potato chip endorsement, opening your own car dealership, or finding out the kid isn't yours. At some point, all of these will happen, and it will to be impossible to hold back your excitement. If you write a song or album about jubilation, hammer the point home with the triple exclamation point.

Exclamation Point Guide:

! = Not believable
!! = Looks like a typo
!!! = OH MY GOD / NO F'ING WAY / YOU'VE GOT TO BE
      KIDDING ME / I DON'T KNOW WHETHER TO CRY, SCREAM,
      OR CURL UP IN THE FETAL POSITION

THE ALBUM'S COVER SHOT IS ALWAYS MORE IMPORTANT THAN ITS CONTENT

Industry execs and radio personalities might have you thinking that sound is what drives sales, but truthfully it doesn't matter what the hell you record on your album. So what makes a Platinum record? The cover art. As long as the lead singer's face takes up the majority of the cover, your fans will be too busy petting his picture to hear what's coming out of the speakers.

Note: If your album really sucks, include a mini pullout poster of the singer in a cowboy outfit.

EVERY ALBUM COVER MUST INCLUDE COLORED SMOKE AND FIRE

Perfect Album Cover Example:

Focal point: The lead singer wearing a top hat and riding a growling leopard

Hidden detail: Lightning reflecting in both the singer's and the leopard's eyes

Background: Purple smoke and fire overlaying a vague glimpse of the Milky Way galaxy

EVERY SINGLE SONG YOU WRITE SHOULD REVOLVE AROUND ONE OF THREE THINGS:

SEX, HAPPINESS, OR CARS

ALWÄYS USË EXCËSSÏVË UMLÄÜTS IN SÖNG TÏTLËS

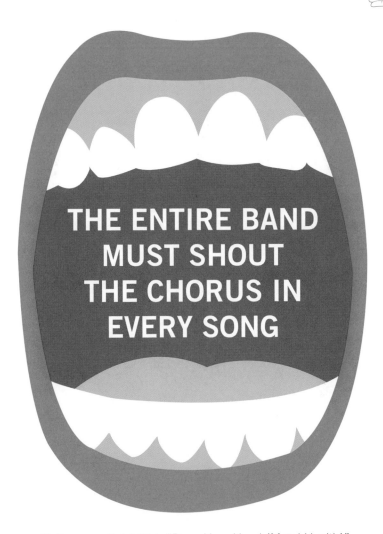

Reference: Quiet Riot, "Bang Your Head (Metal Health)"

THINGS TO BUY WITH THE MONEY FROM YOUR FIRST TOUR:

1. Salon
2. Four identical Italian sports cars, just because you can
3. Pet zebra named Scott
4. Thirty-foot bronze statue of yourself for the center of your backyard
5. Crossbow with custom animal-print graphics
6. Pirate ship
7. Russian figure-skating coach
8. White-bellied Sea Eagle (to perch on your shoulder during pirate ship parties)
9. Implants, as needed

UNDERSTAND THAT
EVERY GROUPIE WILL
SMELL LIKE A UNIQUE
COMBINATION OF
CHAMPAGNE AND
ASHTRAY, REGARDLESS
OF AGE OR LOCATION

**ONLY TWO
AUTOMOBILES
ARE ACCEPTABLE
TO BE SEEN IN:**

**A LIMOUSINE
(WITH A BUILT-IN JACUZZI)
OR A RED FERRARI**

DRIVE A MOTORCYCLE DOWN SUNSET BOULEVARD DAILY

Some people might think you're a candy ass because of your wardrobe, skinny physique, soft voice, and perfect eyebrows. Consequently, to silence your critics, you need to own a motorcycle to show your tough side. Make sure to cover your entire body (while still exposing a little chest, of course) in colored riding leathers before you hop on your Harley.

Note: Avoid biker bars at all costs. Accidentally walking into one will not end well.

ONLY THREE LIQUIDS ARE ACCEPTABLE TO DRINK: VODKA, BEER, AND DIET SODA

Most of the time you'll drink vodka and beer, but if you're too hung over for either, your only option is diet soda. It'll keep you skinny and hydrated and possibly earn you an endorsement deal if you drink it in public.

Remember: Getting fat is the fastest way to commit career suicide and end up working at a music store, so be sure to balance the three appropriately.

LIVE IN LOS ANGELES

Warm weather, abundant sunshine, hot chicks, hot chicks in bikinis, hot chicks working the drive-thru, hot chicks working construction . . . Los Angeles is heaven on earth for the rich and famous. Live there and you'll have endless inspiration for new material, while staying in the spotlight around the clock.

Recommendation: Even though the rent is cheap, it's probably a good idea to stay away from South Central.

BAND LOGOS MUST USE BOLD, SHARP TYPOGRAPHY

Gone are the days of trippy and medieval lettering. Current bands use razor-edged typefaces. If your logo doesn't look like it could cut, impale, or decapitate someone, it's not sharp enough.

Logo Breakdown

Key

1. The sharp, deadly, pointed edge

2. The extreme weight of the logo crushing down

3. The razor-sharp "L" and "W" to cut through a diamond

ALL GUITARS MUST HAVE CUSTOM GRAPHICS

Each axe should match the guitarist's outfit. Solid colors are only allowed if they're neon and coated with a sparkly finish.

Reference:

COLOR KEY:

1. **Wet 'n' Wild:** references your "jungle man" persona

2. **Midnight Lightning:** shows that, like lightning, you are a natural wonder

3. **Fenced In:** reminds everyone that your talent cannot be contained

4. **Heartbreaker:** lets your fans know that you don't care about anyone but yourself, which curiously makes you way more desirable to chicks

ALL LEAD SINGERS SHOULD LOOK LIKE A CHICK FROM BEHIND

Always make sure to get a 360-degree view of groupies before you aggressively grab their ass or lick their neck backstage. Odds are it's your lead singer, which could lead to getting kicked out of the band, emotional scarring, or worse.

So hot, right? WRONG.
This is your lead singer.
Remember to always get
the full 360-degree view
before you make your move.

HIRE THE LEAD SINGER
ON LOOKS ALONE

The vocalist is the face of the band. If he looks like crap, you sound like crap. Don't worry about how terrible his voice is—that can be fixed through coaching, vocal processing, experimental European surgery, and lip-synching. Beauty, on the other hand, can't be taught*; it just is.

*But it can be bought.

NEVER FIRE YOUR LEAD SINGER, NO MATTER HOW MUCH OF A DICK HE IS

Even though he has a Napoleon complex, complains more than your grandma, hits on your girlfriends, is overly emotional, threatens you, swipes your hair spray and shaving cream, never flushes the toilet, drinks all the juice boxes backstage, and accuses you of being attracted to him, the fact is that your band, fame, and finances can't live without your lead singer.

ONLY TWO AREAS OF YOUR BODY ARE ALLOWED TO HAVE HAIR: SCALP AND ARMPITS

THE LEAD SINGER
MUST ALWAYS TALK
IN THE THIRD PERSON*

*Except to bandmates and doctors

THE LEAD SINGER GETS HIS OWN ANNUAL CALENDAR

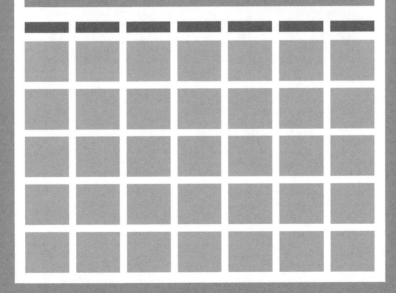

Note: Photos for two of the months must show his bare ass.

IF YOUR NAME DOESN'T SOUND LIKE IT BELONGS IN A LIBRARY, CHANGE IT

REAL NAME	STAGE NAME
Timmy Long	Timothy Long VI
Frank Cage	Franklin Churchill
Chad Roberts	William Landcaster

BASS PLAYERS MUST SWEAR BY "THE BASSIST OATH" BEFORE JOINING THE BAND

Being the bass player of a band is actually as easy as it looks. If you believe it's your true calling, all you have to do is take an oath that will govern the rest of your life. Breaking any of these rules will lead to instant removal from the band and an indisputable forfeit of royalties and rights.

The Bass Player Oath:

As the bassist of my band, I understand that I may never:

- Complain about anything
- Get upset when my tracks are re-rerecorded by the guitarist
- Start my own band in which I sing and/or play guitar
- Get first, second, or third dibs on chicks backstage
- Turn up my amplifier louder than level three
- Voice my opinion
- Look the lead singer in the eye

As the bassist of my band, I understand I must:

- Make at least 80 percent less than the lead singer
- Share my tour bus, clothes, airplane seats, and meals with the roadies
- Keep my mouth shut
- Do everything in my power to remain the most unattractive member of the band

Exemption: Nikki Sixx. He's exempt from every bassist rule in this text.

DRUMSTICKS
NEED TO BE COLORED,
BE CLEAR, OR
HAVE RIBBONS ATTACHED

DRUMMERS MUST ALWAYS WEAR GLOVES

Rough and callused hands belong on masons and mechanics, not rock musicians. Wear gloves while drumming to keep your hands soft and prevent your manicure from getting ruined.

Glove Options:

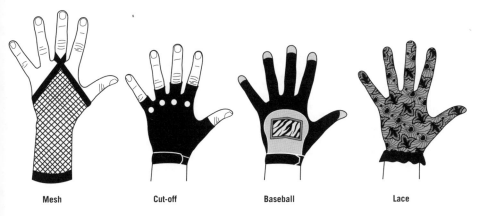

| Mesh | Cut-off | Baseball | Lace |

FOLLOW PROPER PHOTO SHOOT ETIQUETTE

1. Stare directly into the camera lens.

2. Maintain perfect posture at all times.

3. Look really mean and threatening—don't smile.

4. Dramatically shift weight from one hip to the other in between shots.

NEVER CONDUCT A TV
INTERVIEW WITHOUT
SUNGLASSES, CIGARETTES,
PROPER LIGHTING, AND
A BLOOD ALCOHOL CONTENT
OF AT LEAST 0.19

REGARDLESS OF HOW MUCH
MONEY YOU ARE OFFERED,
NEVER PLAY AT STURGIS

NICKNAMES ARE NEVER ACCEPTABLE

CRUDE LIGHTNING SYMBOLS ARE PROHIBITED— USE REALISTIC REPRESENTATIONS ONLY

The symbolic lightning bolt has been around for thousands of years. This, combined with the fact that it was used in every band's artwork in the '70s, is why you should shy away from the mystical emblem.

On the other hand, realistic interpretations of lightning work perfectly on everything imaginable.

Lightning Graphic Reference Sheet

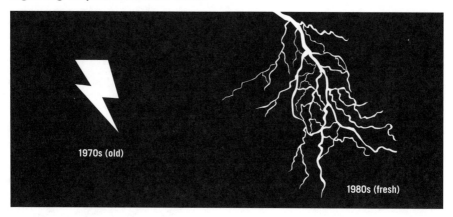

1970s (old)

1980s (fresh)

A PHOTO STUDIO
IS ALWAYS
MORE IMPORTANT
THAN A MUSIC STUDIO

NEVER HEADBANG

1. You'll mess up your hair.
2. You'll get sweaty.
3. You'll give yourself a neck owie.

BEER CANS AREN'T FOR DRINKING FROM— THEY ARE FOR SMASHING, SPRAYING, AND THROWING AT PEOPLE WHO LOOK AT YOU WRONG

STEEL RAINBOW

THE LEAD SINGER SHOULD NEVER BE SEEN IN PUBLIC WITHOUT THE COMPANY OF THREE CHICKS

Note: Being seen with one chick is acceptable only if she's a supermodel, an actress, or a prostitute.

NEVER LET THE DRUMMER GIVE AN UNSUPERVISED INTERVIEW

What's the quickest way to drop a nuke on your musical career? Letting the drummer give an interview on his own. Odds are he'll tell band secrets, threaten everyone in the room with a shank, and make up a rumor about how the band is going to break up. You, and everyone involved with your band, will spend the next three months doing damage control.

If a magazine wants to interview him individually, don't let it happen without a lawyer, three PR people, two security guards, and a tranquilizer gun in the room with him.

Note: It's also recommended you require your drummer to wear a shock collar at all times. This will really help calm down the day-to-day problems.

DRUMMER SUPERVISION CHART

	LAWYER	PUBLICISTS	SECURITY GUARDS	TRANQUILIZER GUN	HIS MOM	K-9 ATTACK DOGS
MTV		X	X	X	X	
Radio Station	X	X	X	X	X	X
News Network	X	X		X	X	
Sci-fi Publication			X	X		
Music Publication	X		X	X		X
Afternoon Talk Show		X	X	X	X	

THE ENTIRE BAND MUST BE TAN, REGARDLESS OF GEOGRAPHICAL LOCATION OR TIME OF YEAR

EACH BAND MEMBER GETS A SIGNATURE COLOR

From the crew of the USS *Enterprise* to the X-Men, every great group in the history of mankind has given its members a signature color. Picking colors should be one of the first things you do as a band. Think long and hard about what you want, because you'll be stuck with it until your third album.

Color Selection Order:

1. Lead singer
2. Lead guitarist
3. Drummer
4. Rhythm guitarist
5. Bassist (told his color by the rest of the band)

II.
STYLE GUIDE

Get ready for the most important fact you will learn in this entire document: *How you look is way more important than how you sound.* This is now considered the cardinal rule of rock 'n' roll. You could be the greatest musician in the world, but no one will buy your music if you look like a drifter from Oklahoma. Remember this one rule of thumb: If you look great, you sound great.

That said, this is obviously the most important section of this guidebook.

HIRE A FORMER PAGEANT WINNER AS YOUR WARDROBE CONSULTANT

DON'T BE SEEN
IN PUBLIC
WITHOUT MAKEUP
ON YOUR FACE

If you don't have the time or resources to apply everything listed on page 4, throw on lipstick and eye shadow at the very least.

PANTS SHOULD ALWAYS BE VACUUM-SEALED TO LEGS

Proper Pants Tightness

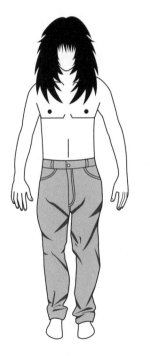

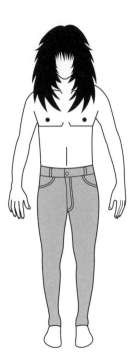

Too Loose   **Ideally Clenched**

CLOTHING FEATURING A FLAG IS COOL, AS LONG AS IT'S NOT AN AMERICAN ONE

Wearing a piece of clothing featuring a European flag gives you a sophisticated "man of international prowess" look. But you'll appear the exact opposite if your outfit displays the American flag. You'll instantly lose all credibility and end up looking like a member of the Charlie Daniels Band.

THE LEAD SINGER CAN ONLY WEAR T-SHIRTS WITH HIS FACE ON THEM

STEEL
RAINBOW

ONE BAND MEMBER MUST WEAR ASSLESS CHAPS DURING PUBLIC APPEARANCES

WHETHER PLASTIC OR
JEWEL-ENCRUSTED GOLD,
NEVER LEAVE HOME
WITHOUT YOUR JEWELRY

ACCENTUATE YOUR FIGURE WITH A DECENT PAIR OF HIGH-HEELED BOOTS

High heels make you look taller, thinner, and generally more attractive. All members—sans the drummer—need to own a few pairs of four-inch heels.

WEARING UNDERWEAR IS NOT COOL—UNLESS YOU'RE SURROUNDED BY OLD WOMEN

EMBRACE SPANDEX

Wearing spandex is a must, especially if you're the lead singer. Not only is it skin-tight and makes your bulge look great, it expands up to six hundred times its size.* That means you'll be able to roundhouse kick, triple axel, and do splits without any restriction.

*Not an exact number, but it sounded believable. Seriously, just buy some spandex already.

ALL HAIR MUST BE TEASED

What separates you from the guys tailgating outside of your arena? Unparalleled hair. Once your locks are about two feet long, follow these steps to have the best hair in a three-hundred-mile radius:

What You'll Need:

- Fifty minutes' prep time
- Hair straightener
- Two cans of hair spray
- Combs (as many as possible)
- Six-pack of Schlitz

How to Properly Tease Hair:

1. First, straighten all hair.
2. Next, grab a two-inch section of hair with one hand.
3. Hold section straight up, and douse with hair spray.
4. Comb section backwards, down toward scalp.
5. Shower section with hair spray again.
6. Grab another two-inch section of hair and repeat steps 3 through 5. Repeat on all hair.
7. Cover face and distribute half a can of hair spray over entire head.

HAIR HEIGHT GUIDE

8'

7'

6'

5'

4'

SMALL: 6–inch   **MEDIUM: 8-inch**   **LARGE: 12-inch**

62

IF YOU ARE GOING TO WEAR A WATCH, WEAR THREE

Exception: Pocket watches. Wear nine.

HEADBANDS
ALWAYS GO UNDER THE BANGS
AND SHOULD BE A MINIMUM OF
TWO INCHES IN WIDTH

ALL JEANS MUST BE RIPPED, FRAYED, STAINED, OR FULL OF HOLES

Note: If you can't find the proper jeans, go downtown and trade pants with a hobo.

ALWAYS MATCH YOUR LIPSTICK TO YOUR SHOES

GUITARISTS, PICK TWO: FAST, BEAUTIFUL, SENSITIVE

When it comes to being a guitarist, it's not like anyone will ever top Hendrix or Clapton, so why put in tons of effort if you don't have to? Celebrity guitarists just need to be two of the following: fast, beautiful, or sensitive.

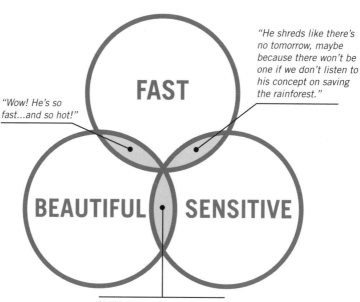

"He shreds like there's no tomorrow, maybe because there won't be one if we don't listen to his concept on saving the rainforest."

"Wow! He's so fast...and so hot!"

FAST

BEAUTIFUL

SENSITIVE

"I didn't even hear any music during the show. His eyes had me in some kind of hypnotic trance."

HANG FOUR TO EIGHT SCARVES FROM YOUR BELTLINE

Scarves around the neck? So '60s.

Scarves around the microphone stand? So '70s.

Scarves around the hips? So enticing.

Note: Only wear red scarves with your matador costume.

NEVER WEAR EARRINGS LESS THAN TWO INCHES IN LENGTH

RULES FOR WEARING COWBOY BOOTS

1. The entire boot must be exposed.
2. They must be snakeskin.
3. They must have spurs.
4. They must double as tap shoes.

NEVER WEAR AN UNTATTERED PIECE OF CLOTHING

Crisp clothing is perfect for church and the office, two places you'll never find a rock star. Every piece of clothing you wear (sans spandex) should be frayed, ripped, stained, acid-washed, stitched, sequined, or shredded.

Style tip: If some clothes are not tattered enough, simply run them over with a lawn mower.

KEEP ATTENTION ON YOUR FACE BY WEARING SOMETHING AROUND YOUR NECK

Between your hair, bare chest, and stuffed pants, your face can easily get lost in the halo of beauty. This can be especially frustrating after you just paid a ton of money to have reconstructive chin surgery. Throwing an accent around your neck will instantly make your face the focal point.

As with lipstick, try to match your neck accent to your shoes:

Shoes	Neck Accent
Cowboy boots	Handkerchief
High heels	Leather choker
Barefoot	Shark tooth necklace or turquoise pendant

IF YOU MUST WEAR A T-SHIRT, SAVAGELY RIP OFF ITS SLEEVES, NECKLINE, AND LOWER HALF FIRST

Not Enough Skin

Perfect

BLACK CLOTHING IS PROHIBITED

Exceptions: Assless chaps and mesh anything.

STEEL
RAINBOW

TWO MEMBERS OF THE BAND MUST WEAR FINGERLESS GLOVES AT ALL TIMES

WEARING A SUIT JACKET IS ONLY ALLOWED IF IT IS SILK, SEQUIN, OR ANIMAL PRINT

Note: Wearing a suit jacket—even the ones listed above—is never allowed at any formal event or award show.

TUCKING IN SHIRTS
IS MANDATORY

One of the biggest fashion faux pas you can commit is to walk around in an untucked shirt. Not only does it make you look like an average person, it covers your crotch.

Tip: No piece of clothing should cover more than the waistline's top inch.

WHITE LINEN PANTS ARE THE ANSWER

If you're in a rush and don't have the time to find your matching spandex, you can't go wrong with white linen pants. Lightweight, see-through, and breathable, these trousers are a gift from the heavens. From making a beer run to practicing karate in your backyard, these versatile pants are ready for any occasion.

Reminder: Even though they are transparent, the no-underwear rule still applies.

WEAR ALL BELTS OUTSIDE THE LOOPS

Your pants will be vacuum-sealed to your body, which eliminates the need for a belt. But if you really want to accent your outfit anyway, you'll need to find one that's seven sizes too big. Ideally, it will drape loosely over your package.

Note: The only belt allowed inside the loops is a Western-themed gun holster.

Dad Belt   **Kenny Rogers Belt**   **Rock Star Belt**

III.
TECHNIQUES

So now you look beautiful. Congratulations! You have the most important part of being a rock star covered. Now on to technique. Luckily for you each instrument has several tricks that are relatively easy to pull off yet look extremely complicated.

Mastering and implementing these techniques is crucial. Everything you learn in this section should be showcased on stage or in music videos. These special moves will wow your fans and turn their focus to the visual spectacle on stage. Their minds will easily be blown away by your tapping-infused solo or consecutive drumstick twirls.

LEARN THE KEY PARTS OF THE ELECTRIC GUITAR

Use the graphic to the right to memorize the important areas of an electric guitar. This will help you understand this section's instructions.

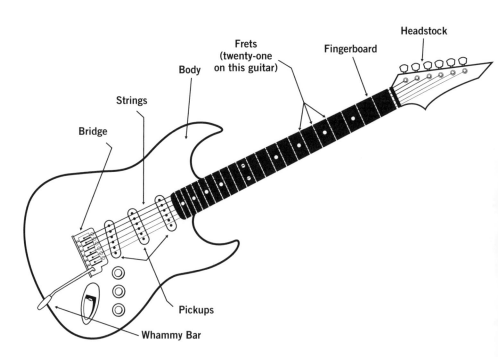

Headstock

Frets
(twenty-one
on this guitar)

Fingerboard

Body

Strings

Bridge

Pickups

Whammy Bar

TAP DURING EVERY GUITAR SOLO

Tapping is an easy way to sound way faster than you really are. Eddie Van Halen popularized this two-handed technique when he recorded "Eruption" (0:57–1:24). Music fans expect to be blown away by every solo, which can put a lot of stress on you, the guitarist. Therefore, never play a solo with less than five seconds of tapping.

Tapping Instructions—Right-Hand Technique:
Start by placing your left index finger on any fret and on any string. Keep this finger anchored down the entire time.

1. First note: Use right index finger to tap (hammer-on*) any fret of the chosen string your left index finger is on.

2. Second note: Pull right index finger up and off the string.

3. Third note: Use middle, ring, or pinky finger on left hand to hammer-on any fret on the string.

4. Repeat steps 1 through 3 as fast as possible. Remember to always keep your mouth open while tapping.

*Hammer-on is defined as quickly bringing a finger down on the fingerboard, which causes a note without picking a string.

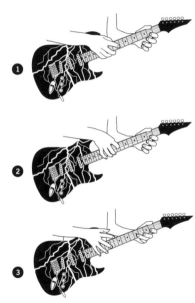

GUITAR HEADSTOCKS SHOULD LOOK LIKE DEADLY WEAPONS

Round, soft, and symmetric headstocks are for pop musicians and washed-up rock stars. Your headstock needs to be razor sharp for three reasons:

1. It looks cool.

2. It shows what a trendsetter you are.

3. It doubles as a dagger that'll intimidate critics, bandmates, and stalkers.

Dull

Deadly

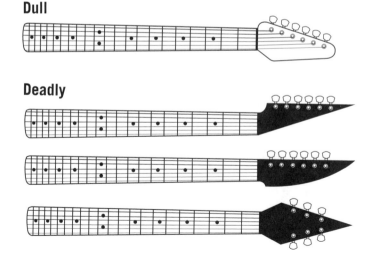

PLAY THIN, LIGHTWEIGHT GUITARS

A thin guitar is extremely mobile and perfect for playing while dancing on stage. Its light physique also means it won't be too heavy to hold for three hours while performing, reducing fatigue and potential back problems.

Note: Playing a custom V (see page 90) is also acceptable.

SPICE UP SONGS WITH
A FEW PINCH HARMONICS

Pinch harmonics are the only thing in the world that can outsqueal your lead singer. This technique is quite simple but takes some practice to perfect. The key is to touch a string with your pick and thumb at the same time.

Instructions:

1. Choke up on the pick (Fig. 2) so only the tip is exposed. This will force your thumb to touch the string simultaneously with the pick.

2. Pick any string.

3. Remove thumb from string immediately after contact, as holding it there will muff the note.

Reference: Van Halen, "Panama" (0:28–0:30)

Pinch Harmonic Pick Hold

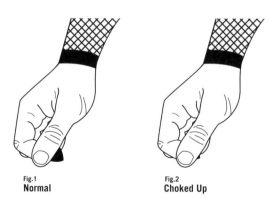

Fig.1
Normal

Fig.2
Choked Up

FINISH EVERY SOLO WITH A DIVE BOMB

A dive bomb is the cherry on top of a tasty solo. This technique utilizes the whammy bar to lower the pitch of a note. Ending each solo with one creates a smooth transition to the chorus and, well, just sounds awesome.

Instructions:

1. After shredding your solo, pick the low E (top) string once.

2. Slowly push the whammy bar down.

3. Once it's all the way down, hold it there for a few seconds.

4. Quickly release and begin playing the chorus.

Note: A dive bomb can be performed with any string, but it just sounds the best using the low E. Additionally, chicks love it when guitarists simultaneously mouth their dive bombs while performing them, so be sure to employ this secret trick.

Reference: Van Halen, "Eruption" (0:38–0:45).

Additional reference: Twisted Sister, "We're Not Gonna Take It" (2:25–2:26). Also, take note of the extensive whammy bar used throughout the entire solo.

MANDATORY:
ONE BAND MEMBER
(PREFERABLY THE
GUITARIST)
MUST BE ABLE
TO PLAY THE SYNTH

DOUBLE-NECK GUITARS ARE SO 1974, SO GET CRAZY AND PLAY ONE WITH FIVE

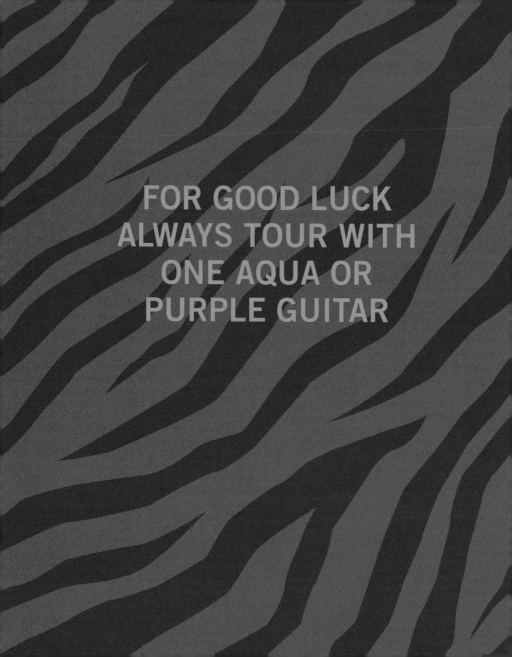

FOR GOOD LUCK
ALWAYS TOUR WITH
ONE AQUA OR
PURPLE GUITAR

EXECUTE THE FERRIS WHEEL AT EVERY SHOW

The "Ferris Wheel" is one of those easy tricks that really gets the crowd all hot 'n' bothered. Before executing this move you'll want to invest in a good pair of strap locks. The last thing you need is a lawsuit because your guitar flew into the crowd and broke some chick's nose.

1. Forcefully push the bottom of your guitar over your shoulder.

2. Maintain perfect posture while the guitar is behind you.

3. Catch guitar.

4. Continue to play, acting like nothing happened.

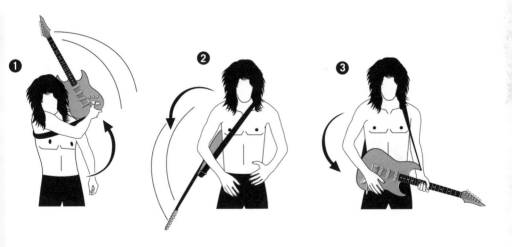

PLAYING A V-SHAPED GUITAR IS ALLOWED, BUT ONLY IF IT HAS A CUSTOM BODY

Streamlined, pointy, and lightweight, V-shaped guitars scream rock 'n' roll. But since they were so popular in the '60s and '70s, playing one is kind of tricky because you don't want to appear out of date. Avoid looking like a member of Bad Company by customizing its shape and color.

Note: Pick guards are prohibited.

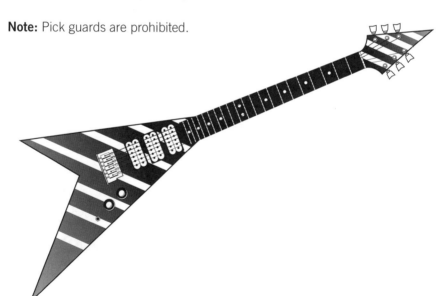

ADD COLOR TO DIFFERENT KEY AREAS OF THE GUITAR

They say the world is your canvas, whatever that means. Rock star interpretation? The guitar is your canvas. To push your look to the limit, add color to every part of the guitar besides the fingerboard.

Use the illustration below like a coloring book and create the raddest-looking guitar ever. The more colors you use, the better.

ONLY PLAY WITH CRYSTAL GUITAR PICKS*

*Diamond, ruby, or jade are okay, too.

PLAY A GUITAR WITH AN UPSIDE-DOWN HEADSTOCK TO GIVE THE IMPRESSION YOU KNOW ROCK HISTORY

The greatest guitarist in history, Jimi Hendrix, was a lefty that played the righty guitar upside down. You've probably never heard of the guy, which is fine, but you need to at least make it appear as though you have. Gain instant credibility by playing a guitar with his signature upside-down headstock.

When people see the Hendrix reference, they'll probably ask you a few questions about his influence on you. Memorize the answers below to avoid blowing your cover.

Common Hendrix Questions, and the Appropriate Answers:

Q. What's your favorite Hendrix album?

A. *Electric Ladyland*

Q. When did you get into Hendrix?

A. Around the age of two. I could actually play "Purple Haze" on a baby guitar before I learned how to walk.

Q. Is your style influenced by Hendrix?

A. I'd say he's my biggest influence, predominately his blues work.

Q. What's your favorite Hendrix song?

A. "Bold as Love"

Other Facts You Should Know:

- Hendrix was from Seattle.
- He died in London at the age of twenty-seven.
- He built his own recording studio called Electric Lady Studios.
- He played with Little Richard before starting his own band.

KEEP IT EASY:
PALM MUTE THE ENTIRE SONG

As you've probably gathered by this point, if you are extremely attractive, odds are you can get away with some lackluster chords and riffs. Luckily, it has been proven that you can have an international hit by only repeating one note the entire song . . . as long as said note is palm muted.

Instructions:
Anchor the side of your hand next to the bridge of the guitar so the strings are—you guessed it—muted. From there, pluck. Boom! You've mastered the elusive palm mute. Combine with good vocals, simple drumbeats, and a few sound effects, and you'll be on your way to the top of the charts.

Simple palm-mute reference: Kiss, "Lick It Up"

Normal Hand Location   **Palm Mute Hand Location**

DRUMS

EACH SET NEEDS TWO TO FOUR BASS DRUMS

Realistically, you can only use two bass drums at a time, but that doesn't mean you can't have a couple more for decoration. In fact, the more bass drums you have, the more talented you look. Load your kit with them and you'll look like the Mozart of percussion.

HANG THREE TO EIGHT GONGS BEHIND THE DRUM SET

If you're going to tour with a bunch of gongs, don't bore the audience by hitting them with a typical mallet. Get creative and use a replica of Thor's hammer, a dull axe, or even your head.

Note: There should always be some type of explosion or pyrotechnic every time a gong is hit.

A rather minimal drum kit

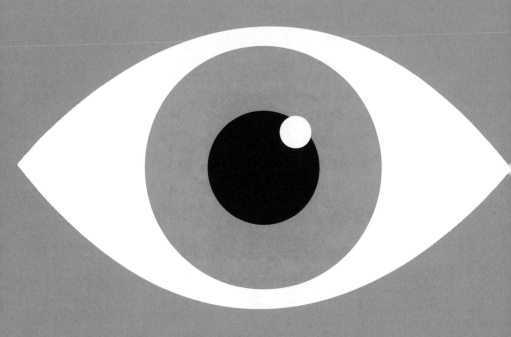

**NEVER DRUM WITH CLOSED
EYES OR MOUTH**

MANDATORY: PLAY THE RIDE CYMBAL DURING THE CHORUS OF EVERY SONG

Reference: Mötley Crüe, "Looks That Kill" (0:44–0:56) or any song recorded from 1980 to 1984

BASS DRUMHEADS MUST DISPLAY A UNIQUE PHOTO

Putting the band logo on a bass drum was only cool in the '60s. At the same time, having a blank bass drum is super boring. Remedy this problem by printing the craziest images possible on bass drumheads.

Good bass drum imagery: California sunset, Jupiter (the planet or the god), creepy yet sexy cyborg chicks, Rick Moranis, jumping dolphins, barbed wire, ice cream sundaes, blonde chicks in aerobics clothes, the lead singer's mom, stallions running on a beach, roses, fruit baskets, Stonehenge, dinner candles, glaciers, or koala bears.

The best image to put on a bass drum? The drummer's face.

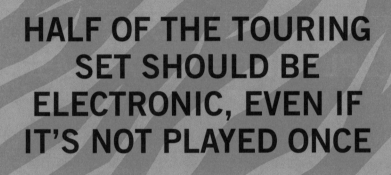

PERFECT THE ART OF PLAYING THE DRUMS WHILE STANDING

HIRE AN INTERIOR DESIGNER TO PROPERLY DECORATE THE DRUM PLATFORM

WEAR
A CAPE
WHENEVER
POSSIBLE

MANDATORY: SURROUND THE SIDE OF YOUR SET WITH A TEN-FOOT CHIME RACK

THERE'S NO SUCH THING AS "TOO MANY CYMBALS"

MOUNT TWO TAMBOURINES TO THE HI-HAT

One tambourine makes you look like a drummer from Jefferson Airplane, while three make you look like you tour with Elton John. Find the happy medium by mounting two tambourines to the hi-hat.

Note: You can substitute three cowbells for one tambourine.

CUSTOMIZE YOUR DRUMSTICKS

Using regular wooden drumsticks is awesome . . . if you're a middle school music teacher. Just like guitars, drumsticks must have custom graphics applied to them. If you're not in the mood for colored wood, use foreign objects that are similar in size.

Paint Job Ideas:

1. Candy cane
2. Midnight lightning (matching your guitarist—how cute)

Custom Ideas:

3. Ninja sai
4. Oversized glow stick

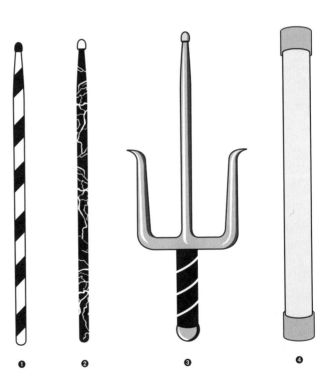

VOCALS

SPEND THE MAJORITY OF EACH DAY WORKING ON YOUR APPEARANCE, OR SLEEPING

INDULGE IN A PAMPER RETREAT ONCE A MONTH

Brain surgeons and commercial pilots have it easy. Being the leader of a famous rock band is the most stressful job in the universe. If you don't take care of yourself, the pressure will cause gray hair, wrinkled skin, and even some weight gain. Avoid these career-ending problems by treating yourself to a pamper retreat once a month. There's no problem in the world a pedicure and chocolate-covered strawberries can't solve.

CARRY ON CONVERSATIONS WITH YOURSELF IN THE MIRROR TO PERFECT THE ART OF GIVING ORDERS AND SPEAKING IN THE THIRD PERSON

CONSTANTLY REMIND YOUR BANDMATES THAT THEY ARE NOTHING WITHOUT YOU

ENROLL IN KARATE, GYMNASTICS, AND CHEERLEADING LESSONS

You'll use techniques from all three while performing live.

Type of Move	Section of Song
Karate	Intro
Gymnastics	Guitar/synth solo
Cheerleading	Outro

PERFECT THE SQUEAL

Looking like a woman will bring you attention, but sounding like one will bring you fame. Spend countless hours perfecting the high-pitched screech—in private and in public—to catapult yourself to stardom.

What's the perfect pitch? Somewhere between a pterodactyl and a cat getting stabbed to death.

COVER ALL OF YOUR INSTRUMENTS WITH DIAMONDS

Lead singer "instruments" include the tambourine, egg shakers, a rainstick, a cowbell, bongos, a triangle, and a woodblock.

LEARN HOW TO OPERATE A FLAMETHROWER

Warning: Before using, first make sure you have at least ten feet of space between you and other band members. Second, no matter the circumstance, never—ever—let the drummer use the flamethrower.

10ft.

SAY "WOOOOOH!" OR "ALLLLLLRIGHT" IN BETWEEN SENTENCES

Note: This applies to both talking and singing.

CREATE AN ONSTAGE ALTER EGO, NAME HIM, AND INFORM THE WORLD YOU ARE NOT RESPONSIBLE FOR HIS ACTIONS

Note: Alter egos are allowed to have nicknames.

Real Name	Stage Name	Alter Ego
Timmy Long	Timothy Long VI	La Fever
Frank Cage	Franklin Churchill	Timmy Doghouse
Chad Roberts	William Landcaster	Rocco

CREATE A SIGNATURE "MOVE"

This is where the karate, gymnastics, and cheerleading lessons really come in handy. Creating a signature move will cement your legacy in rock 'n' roll history. Elvis may be dead, but his hip swivel still lives on today. Once you create a move, repeatedly execute it at every live performance, film session, and photo shoot.

Note: The key is to invent a move with a high success rate. You'll look like a dumb ass if you land on your face following a back handspring off the amplifiers.

Signature Move Ideas:

1. The shooting star
2. The summer swan
3. The heel click
4. The unicorn kick

KNOW YOUR PRIORITIES AND BASE ALL DECISIONS ACCORDINGLY

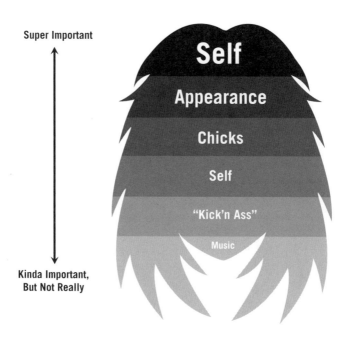

Super Important

Kinda Important,
But Not Really

STAY YOUNG AT ALL COSTS

Fact: Everyone hates an old, washed-up, wrinkly rock star. The older you look, the older your fans feel.

STEEL
RAINBOW

STRETCH DAILY

The last thing you need is a pulled groin from an ill-advised crescent kick. Fans expect to see you running around stage like a Chihuahua on crack. If you're unable to do the splits or jump off platforms, you'll have to cancel shows. Stretch daily to keep your loins loose and prevent injury (which directly translates to lost revenue).

The most important stretch? The Sumo. It's the perfect preshow routine. Follow these simple steps below to ensure groin flexibility.

Sumo Stretch Instructions:

1. Take a deep breath and fully relax body.
2. Slowly squat down while turning feet outward.
3. Lock hands, push inner thighs out with elbows, and hold for ten seconds.
4. Slowly stand up, and take a three-second swig of whiskey.
5. Scream "Yaaaaaaaaaaaaaaa-haaaaaaaaaaa."
6. Repeat steps 1 through 5 three more times.

BASS

STAY OUT OF THE REAL BAND MEMBERS' WAY

DON'T GIVE YOUR OPINIONS OR SUGGESTIONS— NO ONE CARES

DON'T SPEAK
UNLESS SPOKEN TO

REMAIN
THE FATTEST MEMBER
OF THE BAND

ALWAYS REMEMBER: YOU ARE THE MOST REPLACEABLE MEMBER OF THE BAND

Band Hierarchy

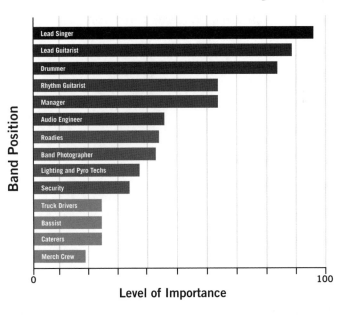

IV.

THE STUDIO

Technically, you can't be an international rock star without a few successful albums. And to do that, you need to dominate the sales charts. The secret to creating a hit album is to give your fans exactly what they want. Your groupies aren't looking for an experimental album about the work of H. G. Wells; they're looking for music that can be blasted in a Camaro, at a backyard barbeque, or in a strip club.

Creating hit songs is like shooting fish in a barrel, so your goal should be to release one radio-friendly album each year. The more hit songs you have, the more money you make on album sales, the more tickets you sell on tour, and the more chicks you get backstage.

INCORPORATE BOTH A SYNTHESIZER AND A GRAND PIANO TO CREATE AN INSTANT RADIO HIT

Song Duration

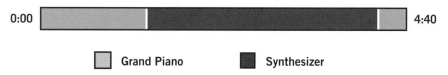

0:00   4:40

■ Grand Piano   ■ Synthesizer

TALK TO YOUR LISTENERS DURING THE SONG'S INTRO

Talking to your listeners during the intro of a song makes them feel special. It lets them know that you actually care about them. Having fans that think they're appreciated will easily increase tour, album, and merchandise revenue.

Ideas:

"How we doing?"

"You better turn this up!"

"This one's for all those people who hate their jobs but need to work to pay their child support or owe their mom rent, man."

"Check this riff out."

"You're looking great tonight, baby."

"Everybody ready for some rock 'n' roll?"

"This one goes out to all the women listening right now."

"Hey, Jeffrey, give 'em a little kick drum."

"We got some gorgeous women out there* tonight, don't we?!"

*In fact, try to include "out there" in every comment.

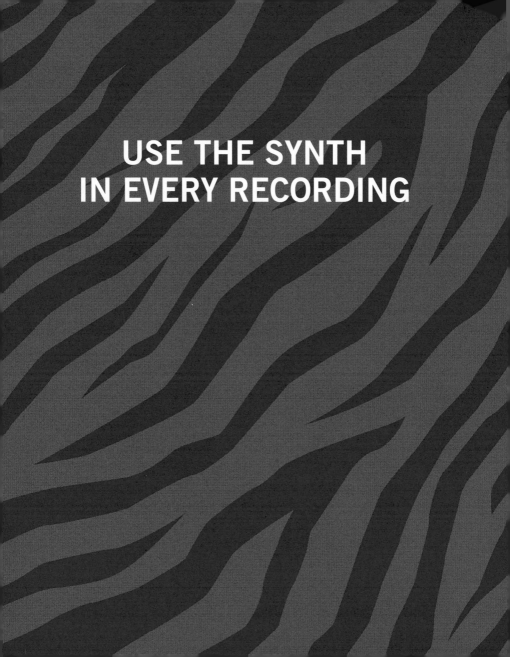

USE THE SYNTH
IN EVERY RECORDING

ADD REVERB
TO EVERY SNARE HIT

Add a gated reverb effect to your drummer's studio recordings. The echoed, whirly result will make any ordinary drum track sound a hundred times cooler.

Reference: Phil Collins, "In the Air Tonight" (3:41–end of song)

**MAKE THE BASS
INAUDIBLE IN EACH SONG**

ONE POWER BALLAD PER ALBUM

Writing an almighty power ballad will catapult you to greatness. This emotional type of song hits home with everyone in the audience, even if the dudes don't admit it. It's a track where you can let it all out: regret, depression, anxiety, self-disgust, the overwhelming feeling of "I don't think I can take this world anymore." This is a place where you can get things off your chest and communicate to your fans how horrible you believe your life is.

Just remember that you can only have one of these per album. Any rock ballad is guaranteed to be a number one hit, which means you'll definitely have to play it at your concerts.

Power Ballad Quick Tips:
- Power ballads should almost always be about love, and ideally, use that word in the title.

- The majority of the ballad should be played with an acoustic or nondistorted electric guitar. However, the guitar solo should always use distortion.

- Never use a synth—only classic pianos will do.

- Incorporating an orchestra is always a good idea.

- The singer needs to sing the initial verses softly. After the first guitar solo, he can really wail away.

- After performing the ballad live, the singer is required to shed a few tears and get choked up while thanking the audience.

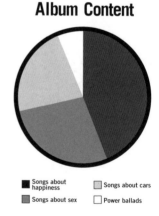

Album Content

- ■ Songs about happiness
- ■ Songs about sex
- □ Songs about cars
- □ Power ballads

IF YOU NEED TO FILL TIME, SIMPLY SCAT

EVERY RECORDING NEEDS TWO OF THE FOLLOWING: WHIPS, WHISTLES, OR A REVVING CAR/MOTORCYCLE ENGINE

EACH SONG REQUIRES TWO LENGTHY GUITAR SOLOS

Song Structure

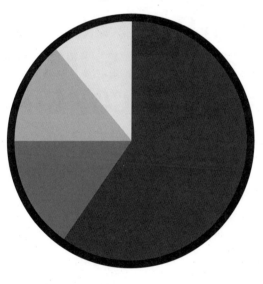

Key

 Guitar Solos
 Lyrics

 Instrumental Intro & Outro
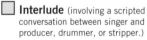 **Interlude** (involving a scripted conversation between singer and producer, drummer, or stripper.)

INCORPORATE AS MANY SOUND EFFECTS AS POSSIBLE INTO EVERY RECORDING

Suggested sound effects include: lasers, feminine laughter, clapping, cigarette inhales, razor blades on a mirror, lip puckers, thunder, whistling (human or wind), tiger growls, popped champagne bottles, swooping airplanes, volcanic eruptions, helicopters, birds singing, electronic chirps and beeps, gentle rain, galloping horses, rocket launchers, someone screaming, "Yes!"

UTILIZE THE CYMBAL CATCH TO PREVENT OVERSHADOWING OF THE GUITAR AND VOCAL PARTS

Loud cymbals are a vital part of every rock song, but sometimes they can over-power the vocals and guitar. Employ the cymbal catch to silence the cymbals and avoid sending the singer into a crazed "I can't hear myself sing because the f-ing drums are too loud again" tirade.

Instructions:

1. Hit the cymbal.
2. Catch and hold the cymbal immediately after contact.

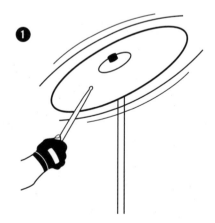
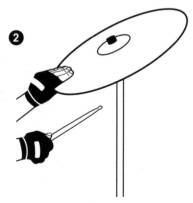

WHILE ADDRESSING YOUR BAND IN A SONG, ONLY REFER TO THEM AS "BOYS"

Example: "Ohhhhhhh yeahhhhhhhhh—haaaaaaaa! Let's go, boys!!!"

THE PERFECT SONG INTRO: PALM-MUTED GUITAR, KICK DRUM, SYNTH HOOK

Start with a single palm-muted riff, and slowly layer the elements on top of each other for the best results.

Intro Progression:

    0:00—Palm-muted riff

    0:16—Kick drum enters

    0:32—Synth hook enters, snare hit enters, lead singer addresses the listeners

    0:48—Lyrics start

Intro Progression

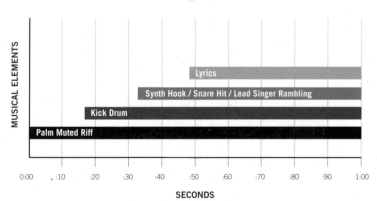

WRITE A SONG FOR ALL
THE PARTY GIRLS ACROSS
THE WORLD, AND MENTION
THEM IN ITS INTRO

WRITE A SONG WITH
"RADIO" IN THE TITLE SO
IT WILL DEFINITELY GET
PLAYED ON THE RADIO

RELEASE A CHRISTMAS ALBUM EVERY TWO YEARS

Note: The album's promotional photo shoot is the only time it's acceptable to wear a scarf around your neck.

USE A TALK BOX ON 50 PERCENT OF THE ALBUM

Thanks to the groundbreaking talk box, lead singers can actually have a solo. Technically, it's so easy even an infant could use a talk box, making this a simple way to please the singer and give your song additional "tech" feel. All the singer needs to do is make sounds with his mouth and the device will do the rest of the work.

Reference: Joe Walsh, "Rocky Mountain Way" (3:10–4:03)

STEEL
RAINBOW

LEAD SINGER: ON THE THIRD ALBUM, WRITE A SONG ABOUT YOUR UNTIMELY DEATH AND HOW MUCH THE WORLD WOULD SUCK WITHOUT YOU

V.

TOUR ETIQUETTE

Easy girls, free drugs, unlimited chocolate, giant hotel rooms with bubble baths and British butlers . . . going on tour is the best part of being a rock musician. But if your shows are boring, you'll have trouble packing arenas (which will dramatically affect the hot-chick-to-decent-chick ratio).

Follow these specific rules and you'll have the greatest show on the planet. To be a successful live performer, you only need to do one thing: Consider yourself more of an entertainer than a musician. Your goal is to become the Siegfried & Roy of music.

ONLY PERFORM AT
SPORTS STADIUMS

Venues to avoid: public access shows, state and county fairs, teenage birthday parties, casinos (sans the Las Vegas Strip), pregame, postgame, and halftime shows, corporate pep rallies, fund-raisers, and professional enrichment conventions.

LEAD SINGERS
ALWAYS NEED TO PERFORM
A STUNT ON STAGE

SMILE THE ENTIRE DURATION OF THE CONCERT

Maybe it's because you are making millions to play music. Maybe it's because there are eight groupies waiting for you backstage. Maybe it's because you just bought your own submarine to easily transfer your cocaine from Mexico without any overhead. Whatever it is, today's rock musicians have absolutely no reason to ever be sad.

Note: If you pass out on stage while performing you are allowed to break this rule, but the second you wake up—whether on stage or in the back of a pickup truck surrounded by chicken cages—you must instantly smile and give a thumbs up.

END THE OPENING SONG WITH A SHOWER OF EMBERS BEHIND THE DRUMMER

CARRY A TRAVEL KIT WITH YOU AT ALL TIMES

Since you can't take your whole vanity on the road, staying beautiful on tour is a challenge. Carry a small travel kit that contains these essentials with you at all times. The case should be portable and fashion forward (see below).

Travel Kit Essentials:

1. Cigarettes
2. Compact mirror
3. Lucky tiger fang
4. Lipstick
5. Mascara
6. Mini vodka bottles
7. Eye shadow

THE LEAD SINGER NEVER WALKS ON STAGE— HE GETS LOWERED FROM THE CEILING OR RAISED FROM THE FLOOR IN A CLOUD OF SMOKE AND LASERS

**SELL PINUPS
OF EACH BAND
MEMBER AT THE
MERCHANDISE
TABLE**

ALWAYS START YOUR SET THIRTY-SEVEN MINUTES LATE AND TELL THE AUDIENCE: "SORRY, DALLAS,* I WAS KIND OF BUSY AND LOST TRACK OF TIME . . . IF YOU KNOW WHAT I MEAN."

*Address the crowd as "Dallas" no matter what city you are in.

THE DRUMMER SHOULD "COBRA" A MINIMUM OF EIGHT TIMES PER SONG

Nicknamed "The Cobra" by some roadie named Bearclaw Michalak, this simple technique reminds the crowd that not all of the awesomeness takes place at the front of the stage. This move can be applied to any song at any time.

To pull off "The Cobra," simply raise your left hand in between snare hits. It's extremely important to keep the beat going with your feet and other hand while performing The Cobra.

Instructions:

1. Hit the snare drum.
2. Raise snare hand as high as possible, and hold until next note.
3. Repeat.

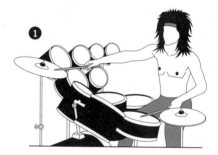

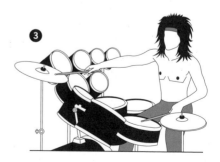

ABSOLUTELY NO DUDES ARE ALLOWED IN THE FLOOR SEATS

Arena Seating Chart

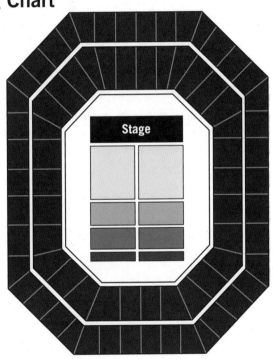

Gorgeous chicks

Decent chicks

Chicks that look good after four drinks.

All other chicks

Dudes and kids

STEEL
RAINBOW

DON'T STEP ON STAGE WITHOUT HALF A BOTTLE OF PEACH-INFUSED VODKA IN YOUR SYSTEM

Note: Don't forget to finish the rest of the bottle during the show.

THE CONCERT STAGE
SHOULD ALWAYS BE
A GIANT REPLICATION
OF THE BAND LOGO

TWIRL ONE DRUMSTICK IN BETWEEN NOTES

Another easy way to draw attention to yourself (and look cool to people who know nothing about playing an instrument) is to twirl one drumstick in between notes. A close relative to "The Cobra," this move requires a little more practice but really drops the jaws.

Technically speaking, this is just an illusion. You're not really twirling the drumstick; you're just rotating it between two fingers. Perfecting this technique automatically makes you an amateur magician. When your music career is over, you could easily work as a street entertainer in downtown Cleveland.

Instructions—Two-Finger Technique:

1. Place the center of the stick in between index and middle fingers.

2. Move both fingers back and forth in opposite directions. This will cause the drumstick to go side to side but not spin.

3. Slightly roll wrist, index, and middle fingers in a clockwise rotation together in unison.

Remember: Coordinating the movement of your fingers and wrist correctly will take some practice. Luckily, this move only requires one hand, so you can use your other one to drink a beer, make a sandwich, or shave your legs.

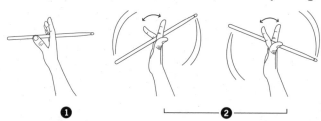

THE DRUMMER IS ONLY ALLOWED TO WEAR A MICROPHONE HEADSET IF HIS DRUM SET SPINS, SWIVELS, ROTATES, OR FLIPS UPSIDE DOWN DURING PERFORMANCES

INVENT A COMMUNICATION SYSTEM TO PICK OUT CHICKS IN THE CROWD

Getting the chick you want backstage is a lot harder than it sounds. Eliminate errors, confusion, and the chance of accidentally hooking up with a cross-dresser by creating a simple communication system between you and the roadies to pluck women from the audience.

The easiest way to do this is to use letters and numbers. Assign each row a letter and each seat a number. The front row is "A" and the first seat on the left of each aisle is "1." So if some chick has been undressing you with her eyes all night and you'd like to get to know her better, count how many rows back and seats in from the left she is. Then tell your roadie, "D-10." It's almost too easy.

THE ONLY TWO MAGAZINES ALLOWED ON THE TOUR BUS ARE *HUSTLER* AND *COSMOPOLITAN*

THE GUITARIST AND
BASSIST SHOULD HAVE
NUMEROUS SYNCHRONIZED
DANCES

THE DRUM SET SHOULD TAKE UP ROUGHLY 50 PERCENT OF THE STAGE

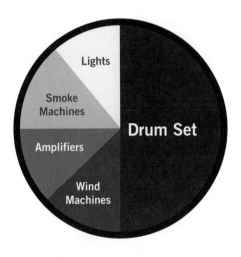

Stage Space

FLASHING
THE ROCK HAND
IS NOT PERMITTED

The rock hand (Fig. 1) is something washed-up '70s musicians
and rebellious teenagers flash. If
you display the symbol on stage,
you'll scare most of your fans out
of the arena. The remainder of
the audience will start burning
chairs and rioting until you play
"Iron Man."

Recommendation: Blow kisses
(Fig. 2) or throw glitter (Fig. 3)
instead.

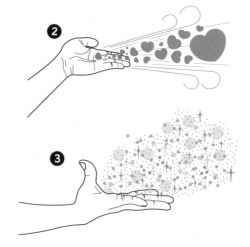

LEAD SINGER: SPIN IN PLACE EVERY FEW MINUTES

Being the lead singer of a band means there will be times when you won't have anything to do on stage. This usually happens during guitar solos. If you're not in the mood to clap your hands, play air guitar, or pretend you're talking to the drummer, just spin in place.

There is no wrong way to spin. Fast, slow, on your back, in the air, with your eyes closed, with your arms out, with your arms in, while snapping your fingers—the possibilities are endless.

Note: If you're too hammered to spin on your own without falling down, standing on a slowly rotating platform is acceptable.

THE LEAD SINGER MAY NEVER USE A MICROPHONE STAND

Exception: If it is used for counterbalance during acrobatics or spun to hypnotize the audience.

ALL BACKUP VOCALS SHOULD BE SUNG WITH ONLY ONE MIC, AND IN ONE OF TWO WAYS

1. Forehead-to-forehead microphone sharing
2. Over the shoulder, cheek-to-cheek microphone sharing

THE LEAD GUITARIST
SHOULD CHANGE GUITARS
AFTER EVERY SONG

ALWAYS END YOUR ENCORES WITH CONFETTI AND GIANT INFLATABLE ANIMALS

THE LEAD SINGER ALWAYS GETS HIS OWN SOLO DURING A SHOW

Solos are a vital part of every concert. It gives the rest of the band a break and allows them to indulge in a few "pick-me-ups" backstage. Each member is entitled to his own solo (yes, even the bassist). Since lead singers don't play an instrument, this can be a problem. Luckily, here are a few simple ideas that will still impress the crowd.

Lead Singer Solo Ideas:

1. **Some type of stunt.** This is the best solution and always gets the crowd excited. Just avoid real lions, jetpacks, and mopeds.

2. **An acoustic cover.** The lead singer should learn one chord on the acoustic guitar and attempt to play some '50s song no one cares about.

3. **Story time.** Dim the lights, bring out a rocking chair, and let him tell a personal "coming of age" story.

4. **Gymnastics.** Roll out monkey bars and mats for a gymnastics routine. Just don't confuse the grip chalk with cocaine.

BEFORE A CONCERT, COVER THE DRUMHEADS WITH GLITTER

A great way to add some dazzle to your live performances is to cover the drumheads with glitter. Every time your drummer hits his drums, you'll have a little sparkly explosion of happiness. **Note:** Never call him Tinkerbell.

EMPLOY SEVERAL "SCOUTS" TO SIFT THROUGH THE CROWD AND GIVE BACKSTAGE PASSES TO HOT CHICKS

You'll be playing in front of twenty-five thousand people every night, making it impossible for you to know how many hot women are in the crowd. This is why you need to employ a legion of chick scouts. They'll go out during shows and look for ladies who want to meet you backstage.

The ideal scout is a tall, relatively unattractive (so as not to get the girls himself), overweight guy who can see over the crowd and knock out a jealous boyfriend if needed. Each scout must also sign a contract that states he will not drink until after the show. This eliminates the threat of beer goggles playing a role in the chick selection.

MULTIPLY THE NUMBER OF AMPS YOU NEED BY SIX

If the audience sees a Sears Tower–size stack of amplifiers, they'll instantly think you're the greatest guitarist ever. Take the number of amps you need and multiply it by six. Then fill the rest of the stage with empty amp cabinets to disguise how many amps you actually are using.

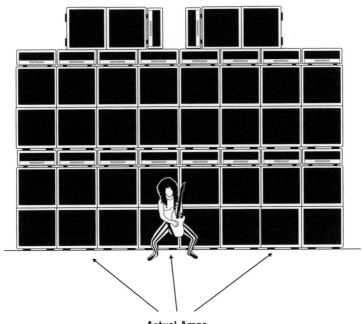

Actual Amps

AIRBRUSH A MESSAGE ON THE BACK OF YOUR GUITAR

Placing a message on the back of your guitar tells the audience you have something important to say. Throw the name of a song, album, girlfriend, sex act, or your hometown on the back of your axe. Then casually flip it up for the crowd to read during guitar breaks or during the lead singer's drunken rambling.

Remember: Always make sure to point to the message and wink or nod.

EACH MEMBER* GETS HIS OWN TOUR BUS

*Except the bass player. He must share with the road crew.

USE UNCONVENTIONAL TECHNIQUES ON THE GUITAR TO "WOW" YOUR FANS

Playing the guitar unconventionally is a simple method that makes the crowd think you're super talented. Just make sure to keep a straight face and act like nothing special is happening.

CONCERT STAGES SHOULD ALWAYS BE WELL LIT

Fans aren't coming to your concerts for just the music. They're coming to see you in person and hoping to flash their way backstage. Stages should be lit to resemble Death Valley at high noon. The majority of the bulb colors should be natural with pink, green, and orange accents.

THE SINGER AND GUITARIST MUST "THREE-WAY" A MINIMUM OF FIVE TIMES PER SHOW

"The Three-Way" (also referred to as "The Tag Team") is when the singer and guitarist play one guitar simultaneously. This trick convinces the audience that the two don't hate each other and allows each woman in the crowd to imagine that she is the guitar, receiving full attention from the two hottest guys on the planet.

There are hundreds of ways to pull off "The Three-Way," but these few rules need to be followed:

1. The two bodies must touch at all times.

2. The lead singer must have a smile on his face, while the guitarist must look completely shocked.

3. Each guy only gets one hand on the guitar.

4. "The Three-Way" cannot exceed one minute in length. It just gets awkward after that.

VI.
MUSIC VIDEOS

A music video is a musician's most powerful self-marketing tool. People can't hear how good-looking you are over the radio. However, they sure can experience love at first sight when they see you on TV.

Music videos provide potential fans with a preview of your live shows, which is why they must follow a specific formula. A great video can take you from playing at bug- and disease-infested clubs to sold-out sports stadiums overnight. While shooting your videos, remember all the things you have learned so far—from fashion tips to techniques—and incorporate them into this section.

HALF OF EVERY VIDEO SHOULD SHOW SCANTILY CLAD CHICKS, WHILE THE OTHER HALF SHOULD SHOW THE BAND PLAYING (WITHOUT AMPS) ON AN EMPTY BLACK STAGE

ALWAYS INCORPORATE A LOW-ANGLE SHOT WITH THE LEAD SINGER SLOWLY CRAWLING TOWARD THE CAMERA

186

DURING HIS SOLO THE LEAD GUITARIST NEEDS TO SPRINT ACROSS THE STAGE AND SLIDE INTO THE CAMERA ON HIS KNEES

FOLLOW THE RULES OF MAKING A VIDEO FROM CONCERT FOOTAGE

Making a music video from concert footage is an easy way to increase ticket sales and avoid two days of filming in a studio. If you want the greatest concert video of the year, follow the shot list below.

Concert Footage Shot List:

1. The band walking on stage in slow motion
2. The singer waving the camera toward him with one hand, while pointing to the crowd with the other and saying, "Wow"
3. Chicks in the crowd crying
4. The singer performing some type of stunt in slow motion
5. A chick lifting up her shirt, then, right before you see anything risqué, a cut to the drummer who mouths "wow" at the camera
6. The bassist (just for one second)
7. The guitarist down on his knees at the end of the stage, melting some chick's face with a solo
8. The band backstage drinking, laughing, and spraying chicks with champagne
9. A closing shot of the tour bus driving into the sunrise with a sign in the back window that reads: "See U Next Year!!!*"

*Be sure to include the triple exclamation point on the sign.

STEEL
RAINBOW

ALL SHOTS OF THE
DRUMMER MUST CONSIST
OF HIM LOOKING INTO
THE CAMERA WITH A
DEER-IN-THE-HEADLIGHTS
EXPRESSION OR
A CREEPY SMILE

EACH MUSIC VIDEO MUST CONTAIN ONE SLOW-MOTION SPLIT KICK OFF THE DRUM PLATFORM

Note: Additionally, all band members must jump off the drum platform in unison when the song begins.

THERE MUST BE THREE WARDROBE CHANGES PER VIDEO

Think of your video as a fashion show. Models don't walk down the runway over and over in the same outfit, so you shouldn't shoot a four-minute video in the same clothes either. Each member must have a minimum of three different wardrobes per video.

Note: The lead singer should have about eleven different outfits.

THROW IN A FEW BLACK-AND-WHITE SHOTS FOR ADDED DRAMA AND ARTISTIC VALUE

USE A WIND MACHINE FOR CLOSE-UPS

IF THE CAMERA IS SOLELY FOCUSED ON ANY OTHER MEMBER, THE LEAD SINGER MUST CRASH THE SHOT

THE GUITARIST NEEDS TO KEEP A CIGARETTE IN HIS MOUTH OR IN HIS GUITAR'S HEADSTOCK THROUGHOUT THE ENTIRE VIDEO

SOMEONE MUST ALWAYS MOUTH, "HI, MOM!"

DON'T START THE SONG EARLIER THAN THIRTY SECONDS INTO THE VIDEO

You can show anything—seriously anything—you want in the beginning of each video, but you may not start the music until you hit the thirty-second mark. From aliens abducting the band to the lead singer paragliding over a redwood forest, the front end of each video is dedicated to showing the most awe-inspiring footage possible.

DURING GUITAR SOLOS THE LEAD SINGER MUST KILL TIME BY FIGHTING AN INVISIBLE PERSON IN THE BACKGROUND

Note: Only use boxing and karate techniques.

BEFORE ANY MEMBER PERFORMS A SPECIAL TRICK OR MOVE, HE MUST FIRST POINT AT THE CAMERA

NO ANCHORED SHOTS ARE ALLOWED—CAMERAS NEED TO SWEEP FROM LEFT TO RIGHT OR ZOOM IN AND OUT THE ENTIRE TIME

If your video doesn't make the viewer a little seasick, it wasn't shot correctly. To get the right amount of movement in your videos, use two cameras. The first camera should sweep back and forth across the stage like a pendulum. The second camera should zoom in and out nonstop, creating a bounce effect. These two techniques will show the world your fast-paced lifestyle.

MANDATORY:
THERE MUST BE THREE
CROTCH SHOTS PER VIDEO

Note: Each crotch should take up 90 percent of the screen for a minimum of four seconds.

CODA

You have now accumulated all the knowledge needed to become a universally famous rock star. Simply reference these rules every day from this point forward and you'll be drinking champagne in your own private helicopter in no time.

Remember that once you've memorized this booklet, it must be destroyed. You have been specifically chosen to learn these secrets because of your good looks, soft lips, and slim physique. If this document slips into the wrong hands, the consequences could be catastrophic—anyone in the world could become a rock star, which may saturate the industry and cause a massive collapse.

Luckily for you, with 1985 right around the corner, this glamorous era of rock has no end in sight. Don't worry if it takes you some time to assemble your band; this guidebook will probably stay relevant for another thirty years. Just make sure that you remain the best-looking person in the group. Remember: The most attractive member automatically and indisputably becomes the leader of the band.

Finally, if you only take away one thing from this document, it must be this: *How you look is always more important than how you sound.* No one will ever shell out half a paycheck to see a bunch of dudes who look like pale, sloppy musicians from Seattle.

Note: If you ever have a question that isn't answered in this booklet, just ask yourself, "What would Cher do?" You'll never make the wrong decision.

ABOUT THE AUTHOR

When most kids his age were listing to sing-alongs, Jordan Hart was getting an education from Led Zeppelin, AC/DC, Van Halen, and Queen—thanks to his dad's album collection. To this day "Panama" remains his all-time favorite song. By the time he was nine, you could argue that he was the world's youngest hard rock scholar. While today he enjoys all kinds of music, classic rock still holds the key to his heart.

A Milwaukee resident, Hart is the creator and writer/editor of 10percentnerd .com, a website dedicated to all of the quasi nerds in the world. He's also a regular guest and the official nerd-world contributor for the Kramp & Adler Morning Show on Milwaukee's FM 102.1. His spare time is spent collecting albums, designing concert posters, playing the drums excessively loud, split kicking off any elevated surface, and shredding on one of his way-too-many guitars. Follow him on Twitter: @Jordan_Hart.